# A Taste of Brazil

## Traditional Brazilian Cooking Made Easy with Authentic Brazilian Recipes

Sarah Spencer

All rights reserved © 2020 by Sarah Spencer and The Cookbook Publisher. No part of this publication or the information in it may be quoted from or reproduced in any form by means such as printing, scanning, photocopying, or otherwise without prior written permission of the copyright holder.

This book is presented solely for motivational and informational purposes. The author and the publisher do not hold any responsibility for errors, omissions, or contrary interpretation of the subject matter herein. The recipes provided in this book are for informational purposes only and are not intended to provide dietary advice. A medical practitioner should be consulted before making any changes in diet. Additionally, recipes' cooking times may require adjustment depending on age and quality of appliances. Readers are strongly urged to take all precautions to ensure ingredients are fully cooked in order to avoid the dangers of foodborne illnesses. The recipes and suggestions provided in this book are solely the opinions of the author. The author and publisher do not take any responsibility for any consequences that may result due to following the instructions provided in this book. All the nutritional information contained in this book is provided for informational purposes only. This information is based on the specific brands, ingredients, and measurements used to make the recipe and therefore the nutritional information is an estimate, and in no way is intended to be a guarantee of the actual nutritional value of the recipe made in the reader's home. The author and the publisher will not be responsible for any damages resulting in your reliance on the nutritional information. The best method to obtain an accurate count of the nutritional value in the recipe is to calculate the information with your specific brands, ingredients, and measurements.

*ISBN: 9798615054297*
*Printed in the United States*

— THE —
**COOK BOOK**
PUBLISHER

www.thecookbookpublisher.com

# CONTENTS

| | |
|---|---|
| INTRODUCTION | 1 |
| BRAZIL'S FOOD CULTURE | 3 |
| APPETIZERS AND SALADS | 7 |
| SOUPS AND STEWS | 27 |
| MAIN ENTRÉES | 45 |
| VEGETARIAN, SIDES, BEANS AND RICE | 73 |
| DESSERTS | 91 |
| RECIPE INDEX | 105 |
| COOKING CONVERSION CHARTS | 109 |

↳ BORING!!

# INTRODUCTION

When you think of Brazil, you probably think of its beautiful beaches, samba dancing, Carnival, skimpy bikinis, Rio de Janeiro—and last but not least, its flavorful cuisines.

Brazilian cooking has gained international popularity thanks to its exotic mix of African, Portuguese and indigenous cuisines. And Brazilian food inspiration does not stop there, as many cultures—primarily German, Middle Eastern, Italian and Japanese—have played their role in influencing many of Brazil's classic cuisines. So although it starts with the indigenous tribes—and usually beans and rice—Brazilian food represents a fusion of many different culinary traditions and food cultures.

That's because Brazil itself represents a melting pot of people and cultures from all over the world. Their love for their food is simply amazing to experience. They love sharing both meals and food stories that have been passed down through many generations of their ancestors. Their cooking techniques reflect the influences of these past immigrants, which have now coalesced in a uniquely Brazilian way.

Amazonian ingredients add a special touch. Locally grown tropical fruits and vegetables make meals wholesome and full of vibrant flavors. Street foods rule the Brazilian heart, and you can find street food stalls in every nook and corner of the streets. Every recipe has something to savor.

Many foreigners assume that cooking Brazilian recipes is a complex and time-consuming task. But while it is true that many of the recipes *sound* exotic, they are actually quite manageable and approachable. Yes, Brazilians eat jungle herbs, tripe and many other unusual local ingredients;

however, their food culture also includes plenty of space for salads, soups, stews, pasta, rice, burgers, and pizza. It also helps that Brazil is a developing country where most food is cooked at home and prepared from scratch. That means that most dishes are *easy* to prepare at home without any special kitchen skills or utensils.

# BRAZIL'S FOOD CULTURE

When you read a Brazilian recipe for the first time, you may find yourself overwhelmed at the thought of having to assemble so many different ingredients. But after a few attempts, you'll find it easy enough to pull them all together. Many supermarkets now sell real Brazilian cheeses, fruits, and other staple ingredients.

### Rice

Rice is a big staple in Brazil and a must-have pantry ingredient if you're interested in cooking Brazilian food. Any long-grain white rice can be used; however, brown rice is a healthy alternative.

### Vegetables

Sautéing is a very Brazilian way of cooking. Many recipes start with sautéing common vegetables such as tomatoes, onions, ginger, and garlic. Zucchini, hearts of palm, okra, cauliflower, carrots, eggplant, squash and pumpkin are also used very frequently.

### Beans

Beans are a classic ingredient in Brazilian cooking. They add protein and flavor to numerous dishes. Pinto beans and black beans are the most popular, so get a few packages of these to store in your pantry.

### Fruits and Nuts

Brazil is known for its spectacular range of tropical fruits. Many of them are not available in supermarkets in other countries; however, some of them can be found in frozen form. Guarana is a naturally caffeinated local fruit that is used in many soda and syrup preparations. Commonly available fruits such as coconut, strawberries, mango, citrus fruits, plantains, bananas, pineapple, papaya, raisins, and olives are all widely used in Brazilian cuisine. Acai berries and passion fruit are more exotic, but you may be able to find frozen passion fruit pulp and acai berries at your local supermarket or health food store. Acai berries especially are known for their health properties and are now being added to many smoothie preparations. In Brazilian cuisine, acai puree is used in many salads and other vegetable dishes.

When it comes to nuts, walnuts, cashews, peanuts and—of course—Brazil nuts are often used in Brazilian cooking.

### Meat

Brazilians simply love eating their local meat cuts! Churrasco is the trademark grilled meat recipe of Brazilian cooking. Chicken, beef, and pork are standard meats used in churrasco preparations. Another specialty of Brazil is its dried beef, which is quite commonly added to many bean and manioc dishes. Brazilian dried beef is often hard to find in supermarkets; however, you can replace it with pastrami or chipped beef.

### Fish and Seafood

Brazil's expansive coastal regions harvest a variety of seafood, but the country actually produces more freshwater fish. Pacu and piraruku are two popular kinds of freshwater fish. Bahian food culture uses dried shrimp in abundance, and another popular seafood ingredient is dried salt cod.

## Cachaca

Cachaca is a popular rum-like liquor prepared from fermented sugarcane juice. It is used in many Brazilian cocktails.

## Manioc

The root vegetable manioc plays an essential role in Brazilian cooking. It is also known as cassava and yuca root. Manioc is one of the commonest ingredients in Brazilian pantries. Yuca flour and yuca starch are also used in a few recipes.

## Sweets

Sugar, condensed milk, chocolate, fruits, and nuts are the core ingredients of popular Brazilian desserts such as rice pudding and milk caramel. Condensed milk is a common ingredient used to prepare Brazilian chocolate truffles. Table cream, a kind of fresh cream, is added to many desserts and milk-based sweets as well as savory cuisines.

# APPETIZERS AND SALADS

## Salt Cod Croquettes (Bolinho de Balcalhau)

*Serves 4–6 | Prep. time 10 minutes | Cooking time 25–30 minutes*

**Ingredients**

2¼ pounds potatoes
17–18 ounces boiled salt cod (skinned and boned)
3 tablespoons freshly chopped parsley
2 egg yolks
1 egg white
1 medium onion, finely chopped
1 garlic clove, finely chopped
Ground black pepper and salt to taste

**Directions**

1. Add the fish to a bowl of cold water. Soak for 24 hours, changing water 3–4 times in between.
2. Boil water in a medium saucepan or skillet.
3. Add the fish and blanch for 10–15 minutes. Cool and drain, reserving the water. Crumble the fish; remove the skin and bones.
4. Heat the reserved water in a medium saucepan or skillet over medium heat.
5. Add the potatoes; stir-cook until tender and soft.
6. Drain and transfer to a bowl.
7. In the pan, heat the oil over medium heat.
8. Add the onion and garlic; stir-cook until soft and translucent.
9. In a mixing bowl, combine the cooked onions, fish, potatoes, egg yolk, egg whites, black pepper, and parsley.
10. Combine into a flaky dough. Season with some salt to taste.
11. Form the dough into small croquettes.
12. Heat the oil in a deep saucepan or frying pan over medium heat.
13. Deep fry the croquettes until golden brown.
14. Drain over paper towels. Serve warm.

***Nutrition (per serving)***
Calories 208, fat 4 g, carbs 22 g, protein 24 g, sodium 186 mg

# Cornmeal Empanadas (Pastel de Milho)

*Yield 32 Pastries | Prep. time 20–30 minutes | Cooking time 35–40 minutes*

### *Ingredients*
Pastry
3 cups all-purpose flour
6 tablespoons unsalted butter, melted
1 tablespoon baking powder
½ teaspoon salt
10 ounces thickened cream
1 tablespoon chilled milk

Egg Wash
½ tablespoon milk
1 large egg yolk

Herb Filling
3 tablespoons extra-virgin olive oil
2 spring onions (scallions), chopped
½ bunch basil, chopped
1 medium onion, chopped
Kernels from 5 small sweet corn cobs
½ teaspoon ground cayenne pepper (optional)
Ground black pepper and salt to taste

*Directions*
1. In a mixing bowl, combine the baking powder, salt, and flour.
2. Mix in the butter and combine until mixed well and crumbly.
3. Add the milk and cream; combine and knead into a ball.
4. Cover and set aside for 30–40 minutes to rise.
5. Heat the oil in a medium saucepan or skillet over medium heat.
6. Add the onion; stir-cook for 4–5 minutes until soft and translucent.
7. Add the corn kernels and stir-fry for 4–5 minutes.
8. Add the cayenne pepper, black pepper, salt, and herbs. Combine well and cool down completely.
9. Transfer the mixture to a blender. Blend to make a smooth paste.
10. Preheat an oven to 350°F. Line two baking dishes with parchment paper.
11. Roll the dough into a 1½-inch-thick layer. Cut into about 30–32 rounds using a pastry cutter.
12. Add 1½ tablespoons of the mixture to each circle. Using wet fingers, bring together the edges to make a semicircular shape and seal the edges by crimping.

13. Place in the baking dishes and bake for about 20 minutes until golden brown.
14. Serve warm with favorite dipping sauce, if desired.

*Nutrition (per serving)*
Calories 109, fat 19 g, carbs 12 g, protein 6 g, sodium 249 mg

# Bahian Style Breaded Shrimp (Camarao Empanado)

*Serves 6 | Prep. time 10 minutes | Cooking time 25 minutes*

*Ingredients*

2 tablespoons annatto oil or corn oil
2 pounds large shrimp, shelled and deveined, tails left on
3 cloves garlic, minced
Juice of 1 lime
2 teaspoons salt (divided)
1 small onion, minced
6 scallions, white and light green parts, minced
½ medium green bell pepper, minced
½ medium red bell pepper, minced
¼ cup tomato sauce
6 plum tomatoes, minced
1 Scotch bonnet or habanero chili, halved and seeded
½ cup unsweetened coconut milk
1 tablespoon cilantro leaves and stems, minced
Lime wedges to serve

*Directions*

1. In a mixing bowl, combine the garlic, shrimp, lime juice and 1 teaspoon of salt. Set aside to marinate for 30 minutes.
2. Heat the oil in a medium saucepan or skillet over medium heat.
3. Add the scallions, bell peppers and onion; stir-cook for 4–5 minutes until soft and translucent.
4. Mix in the tomatoes; stir-cook for 4–5 minutes until softened.
5. Turn heat to low. Mix in the coconut milk, chili, tomato sauce and 1 teaspoon of salt.
6. Simmer the mixture for 8–10 minutes.
7. Increase heat to medium-high. Add the shrimp; stir-cook for 4–5 minutes until pink and opaque.
8. Remove the chili. Top with the cilantro and serve warm with steamed rice and lime wedges.

*Nutrition (per serving)*
Calories 187, fat 6 g, carbs 11 g, protein 38 g, sodium 652 mg

# Cheese Croquettes (Bolinho de Queijo)

*Yields 45 cheese balls | Prep. time 15–20 minutes | Cooking time 20–30 minutes*

### Ingredients
Dough
1¼ cups all-purpose flour
2 cups milk
1 tablespoon salt
3 tablespoons butter
1 ounce grated parmesan cheese

Cheese Balls
1–2 eggs, beaten with a pinch of salt
8–9 ounces stretched-curd cheese, cubed
All-purpose flour as needed

Breadcrumbs and peanut oil as needed

### *Directions*
1. Heat the butter in a deep saucepan or cooking pot over medium heat.
2. Add the salt and milk; heat the mixture.
3. Add the flour and combine well to avoid lumps. Cook until mixed well.
4. Remove from heat, mix in the cheese and combine. Let cool.
5. Knead the mixture to prepare a flaky dough. Divide it into small balls and press them down one by one to make a hollow in the center.
6. Add the cheese cubes in the hollow. Fold the sides up to cover up the cubes.
7. In a mixing bowl, beat the eggs and mix in some salt.
8. In two separate bowls, add some flour and breadcrumbs.
9. Roll the balls first in the flour and then coat with the egg mixture. Lastly, coat with the breadcrumbs.
10. Heat the oil in a deep saucepan or frying pan over medium heat.
11. Deep fry the balls until crispy and golden brown. Drain over paper towels and serve warm.

### *Nutrition (per serving)*
Calories 336, fat 21 g, carbs 23 g, protein 17 g, sodium 1432 mg

# Brazilian-style Potato Salad (Majionese de Patatas)

*Serves 4 | Prep. time 15–20 minutes | Cooking time 10 minutes*

### Ingredients
2¼ pounds potatoes, washed, peeled and cut into 1-inch cubes
1 tablespoon apple cider vinegar
A large pinch of salt, or to taste
¼ large white onion, finely grated
1 cup mayonnaise
1 clove garlic, finely minced or crushed
¼ cup lime juice
2 tablespoons mint leaves, chopped
3 tablespoons cilantro or parsley, chopped
½ cup pitted kalamata or green olives, chopped

3 tablespoons green onions, chopped, plus more for garnish
Ground black pepper to taste
2 large hard-boiled eggs, chopped (optional)
Whole olives for garnish

### *Directions*
1. Boil the potato cubes in water in a saucepan. Add a pinch of salt and keep boiling for 8–10 minutes until the potatoes are tender and soft.
2. Drain and transfer to a mixing bowl.
3. Mix in the vinegar.
4. In another bowl, mix the lime juice, mayonnaise, garlic, chopped olives, grated onion, mint, green onions, cilantro (or parsley), salt and black pepper.
5. Mix in the eggs and potatoes. Refrigerate for 1–2 hours.
6. Serve topped with some chopped green onions and whole olives.

### *Nutrition (per serving)*
Calories 523, fat 26 g, carbs 33 g, protein 6 g, sodium 594 mg

# Tropical Cobb Salad (Salata Tropical)

*Serves 6 | Prep. time 10 minutes | Cooking time 0 minutes*

**Ingredients**
Dressing
¼ cup orange juice
3 tablespoons lime juice
½ teaspoon liquid aminos
⅓ cup chopped cashews
½ cup parsley leaves
½ teaspoon ground black pepper

Salad
1 (14½-ounce) can hearts of palm, rinsed and cut into rounds
8 cups loosely packed mixed greens
1 red bell pepper, diced
1 green bell pepper, diced
½ red onion, thinly sliced in half-rings
1 avocado, diced
1 cup corn kernels, fresh or frozen and thawed
1 cup unsalted and cooked black beans, drained
2 tablespoons cashews

### *Directions*
1. Combine all the salad ingredients using a blender; blend to make a smooth mixture.
2. Season to taste and set aside.
3. Arrange the onion slices in a bowl. Add a few ice cubes on top and set aside for 15 minutes.
4. Drain the water.
5. Add the greens to a serving plate and arrange the remaining salad ingredients in between them.
6. Serve with the prepared dressing.

### *Nutrition (per serving)*
Calories 160, fat 6 g, carbs 25 g, protein 7 g, sodium 330 mg

# Black Eye Pea Fritters (Acaraje de Bahia)

*Serves/Yield 15–20 Fritters | Prep. time 10–15 minutes | Cooking time 70–75 minutes*

**Ingredients**

Cakes
2 cups black-eyed peas
2 cups onions, roughly chopped
Salt to taste
3 cups vegetable oil to fry

Filling
10½ ounces dried processed shrimp
3 ounces unsalted cashews
3 ounces unsalted peanuts
11½ ounces day-old bread
2 tablespoons fresh ginger, peeled and roughly chopped

2 cloves garlic, finely chopped
1 medium onion, roughly chopped
1 red chili, finely chopped
3½ cups unsweetened coconut milk
1 large tomato, roughly chopped
2 tablespoons vegetable oil
Salt and ground black pepper to taste
1 handful coriander, roughly chopped

To serve
2 tomatoes, finely chopped
Handful of coriander, finely chopped
Hot pepper sauce

### *Directions*
1. In a large bowl, add the peas and cold water to cover. Set aside for 24 hours to soak. Drain water.
2. Add the peas and onions to a blender and blend to make a smooth mixture.
3. Transfer the mixture to a bowl and season with some salt. Combine well to make a fluffy mixture.
4. Soak the shrimp in cold water for 30 minutes. Drain and add to the blender.
5. Blend to make a smooth, pulpy mixture.
6. Transfer to a bowl.
7. Add the bread to the blender and blend to make a pulpy mixture.
8. Add the peanuts and cashews and blend for 2 more minutes.
9. Heat the oil in a medium saucepan or skillet over medium heat.
10. Add the onion, ginger, garlic, and red chili; stir-cook for 2–3 minutes until soft and fragrant.
11. Add the pea mixture, shrimp mixture, cashew mixture, and the remaining filling ingredients except for the coriander. Simmer the mixture over low heat for 25–30 minutes. Season with black

pepper and salt. Mix in the coriander; set aside for 10 minutes.
12. Prepare small balls from the mixture.
13. Heat the oil in a deep saucepan or frying pan over medium heat.
14. Drop the balls one by one and fry them in batches for 3–4 minutes per side until they are evenly bright orange and crisp.
15. Drain over paper towels and serve with tomatoes, coriander, and hot pepper sauce as a dip.

*Nutrition (per serving)*
Calories 172, fat 9 g, carbs 17 g, protein 6 g, sodium 176 mg

# Fried Chicken Pastries (Pastel de Frango Com Catupiry)

*Serves 8–10 | Prep. time 10 minutes | Cooking time 20–25 minutes*

*Ingredients*

2 tablespoons cachaca
1 teaspoon apple cider vinegar
3¼ cups + 1 tablespoon all-purpose flour (divided)
¼ cup vegetable shortening
1¾ teaspoons salt (divided)
1 large egg
2 cups + 2 tablespoons vegetable oil
1½ cups cooked chicken breast, shredded
1 teaspoon paprika
1 medium onion, peeled and chopped
2 cloves garlic, minced
1 teaspoon tomato paste
½ cup fresh or frozen corn
½ cup chicken broth
½ teaspoon ground black pepper
2 tablespoons fresh parsley, minced
1 scallion, chopped
¼ pound requeijao cheese

*Directions*

1. In a mixing bowl, combine the 3¼ cups flour, shortening, cachaca, vinegar, egg, 1 teaspoon of the salt and 10 tablespoons of warm water.
2. Knead the mixture into a flaky dough. Wrap and chill in the refrigerator for 30 minutes.
3. Heat the 2 tablespoons of oil in a medium saucepan or skillet over medium heat.
4. Add the onion; stir-cook for 4–5 minutes until soft and translucent.
5. Add the garlic and stir-cook for 1 minute until brown and fragrant.
6. Mix in the shredded chicken, tomato paste and paprika.
7. Add the 1 tablespoon of flour; stir-cook for 1–2 minutes.
8. Mix in the corn and broth; stir-cook to thicken the mixture.

9. Season with the black pepper and remaining salt.
10. Stir in the parsley, cheese, and scallions. Let cool.
11. Roll the dough over a floured surface into a ¼-inch-thick square. Set aside for 5–10 minutes.
12. Cut into 7-inch squares; add 2 tablespoons of prepared mixture to each square.
13. Fold the edges half-diagonally and press them to create a seal.
14. In a frying pan, heat 2 cups of oil.
15. Add the sealed pastries in batches. Fry for 2–3 minutes per side to an evenly golden brown.
16. Drain over paper towels and serve.

*Nutrition (per serving)*
Calories 299, fat 8 g, carbs 36 g, protein 17 g, sodium 298 mg

## Cheese Bread (Pao de Queijo)

*Yields 20–25 balls (4–6 serving) | Prep. time 10 minutes | Cooking time 25–30 minutes*

*Ingredients*

7 tablespoons milk
7 tablespoons vegetable oil
Pinch of salt
1 cup tapioca flour
½ cup parmesan cheese, grated
1 medium egg, beaten

*Directions*

1. Heat the oil in a medium saucepan or skillet over medium heat.
2. Add the milk and salt; boil the mixture.
3. Turn off heat and mix in the flour. Combine well.
4. Mix in the egg and cheese; knead into a flaky dough and shape it into a ball.
5. Preheat the oven to 350°F.
6. Prepare small balls from the dough.
7. Line a baking tray with parchment paper and arrange the balls over it.
8. Bake for 20 minutes, until the balls turn golden and puffed.
9. Serve warm.

*Nutrition (per serving)*

Calories 269, fat 18 g, carbs 20 g, protein 4 g, sodium 197 mg

# Brazilian Chicken Salad (Salpicao)

*Serves 6–8 | Prep. time 10 minutes | Cooking time 0 minutes*

### Ingredients
½ green or red capsicum (bell pepper), julienned
½ pound cold-smoked chicken, shredded
½ small fresh pineapple, cored and roughly chopped
3½ ounces pecans or walnuts, roughly chopped
1½ ounces sultanas (golden raisins)
1 medium carrot, julienned
1 apple, julienned
5 iceberg lettuce leaves, roughly sliced

1 spring onion (scallion), finely sliced
Juice of 1 lime
2 tablespoons mayonnaise
Ground black pepper to taste

### Directions
1. Whisk the black pepper, mayonnaise and lime juice in a mixing bowl.
2. Combine the other ingredients in another bowl. Top with the dressing and serve.

### Nutrition (per serving)
Calories 207, fat 15 g, carbs 11 g, protein 9 g, sodium 377 mg

# SOUPS AND STEWS

## Black Bean Stew with Smoked Meats (Feijoada Completa)

*Serves 8–10 | Prep. time 15–20 minutes | Cooking time 4–4½ hours*

**Ingredients**
½ pound Brazilian dried beef or beef jerky
1½ pounds small black turtle beans, soaked overnight and drained
1 ham hock
1 pound beef sirloin or smoked pork loin
1 pound smoked chorizo or other smoked sausages, spicy
½ pound slab smoked bacon
1 pound pork ribs

½ pound smoked pig (optional)
2 onions, finely chopped
3 cloves garlic, mashed
¼ cup vegetable oil
⅓ cup parsley, chopped
1½ teaspoons cumin
1 bay leaf
Salt and ground black pepper to taste

*Directions*
1. Add the dried beef to a large bowl and cover with cold water. Soak overnight, changing the water every 3–4 hours.
2. Add the beans and enough water to cover to a deep saucepan or cooking pot; heat it over medium heat.
3. Mix in the beef and ham hock.
4. Simmer for about 2 hours, until the beans are cooked well. Discard the ham hock.
5. Mix in the bay leaf and remaining meat. Simmer the mixture for about 25–30 minutes.
6. Heat the oil in a medium saucepan or skillet over medium heat.
7. Add the onion and garlic; stir-cook until soft and fragrant.
8. Season with the salt, cumin, and black pepper. Mix in the parsley.
9. Add the mixture to the meat mixture and simmer for 25–30 more minutes.
10. Cut the meat into small pieces and return it to the mixture.
11. Serve with the orange slices, pepper sauce, collard greens or Brazilian style rice.

*Nutrition (per serving)*
Calories 517, fat 28 g, carbs 15 g, protein 42 g, sodium 706 mg

# Brazilian Beef Stew (Picadinho de Carne)

*Serves 4 | Prep. time 20 minutes | Cooking time 50 minutes*

### Ingredients
2¼ pounds stewing beef, cubed
½ tablespoon onion powder
1 teaspoon salt
½ tablespoon cumin
½ tablespoon garlic powder
¼ teaspoon ground black pepper
3 cloves garlic, minced
2 tablespoons vegetable oil
½ large yellow onion, diced
2 cups beef stock
1 tablespoon red wine vinegar
1 teaspoon annatto powder (optional)

½ medium butternut squash, deseeded and cubed
1 large Yukon potato, peeled and cubed
1 teaspoon tomato paste
¼ cup fresh cilantro, chopped
2 carrots, peeled and sliced

### Directions
1. Season the beef cubes with the salt, pepper, onion powder, cumin, and garlic. Set aside for 30 minutes.
2. Heat the oil in a medium saucepan or skillet over medium heat.
3. Add the onion; stir-cook for 2–3 minutes until soft and translucent.
4. Add the garlic and stir-cook for 30 seconds until brown and fragrant.
5. Add the beef cubes; stir-cook to evenly brown.
6. Mix in the vinegar and stock. Stir and then mix in the annatto and tomato paste.
7. Bring the mixture to boil; turn heat to low and cover. Simmer for 40–50 minutes.
8. Add the squash, carrots, and potatoes; simmer for 15–20 more minutes.
9. Serve with the cilantro on top.

### Nutrition (per serving)
Calories 352, fat 19 g, carbs 33 g, protein 14 g, sodium 1638 mg

# Heart of Palm Soup

*Serves 6–8 | Prep. time 5 minutes | Cooking time 10 minutes*

**Ingredients**
1 cup heavy cream
1 cup parmesan cheese, shredded
4 (14-ounce) cans hearts of palm, drained and sliced
3 cups chicken stock or water
1–2 sprigs fresh herb of choice, for garnish
Salt and black pepper to taste

**Directions**
1. Heat the stock in a medium saucepan or skillet over medium heat.

2. Add the palm hearts and thyme; boil the mixture for 4–5 minutes.
3. Remove the thyme.
4. Transfer the palm hearts to a blender along with the cooking liquid. Blend to make a smooth mixture.
5. Place the mixture in a serving bowl. Mix in the cream and parmesan cheese; serve warm. Garnish with herb if desired.

*Nutrition (per serving)*
Calories 218, fat 16 g, carbs 11 g, protein 9 g, sodium 832 mg

## Leao Veloso Seafood Soup

*Serves 10 | Prep. time 10 minutes | Cooking time 70–75 minutes*

## Ingredients

2 pounds clams or mussels, scrubbed and debearded
1 pound medium shrimp, unpeeled and washed
1 large (3-pound) white fish, whole and with the head (grouper, snapper)
3 cloves garlic, smashed
1 tablespoon cilantro, finely chopped
4 large tomatoes, peeled, seeded and chopped
1 tablespoon sweet paprika
Salt to taste
1 whole chili pepper (malagueta, jalapeno, serrano)
2 medium onions, chopped
½ cup Italian parsley, finely chopped
¼ cup extra-virgin olive oil
1 pound lobster meat, coarsely chopped
1 pound crab meat, picked over
2 quarts water

## Directions

1. Cut the fish head from the body; cut the body into steaks and chop the head into small pieces. Set aside.
2. Add the fish head pieces and 2 quarts of water to a deep saucepan or cooking pot and heat over medium heat.
3. Bring the mixture to boil; turn heat to low. Simmer for 55–60 minutes.
4. Strain the mixture/stock with a cheesecloth.
5. Heat the stock in a deep saucepan or cooking pot over medium heat.
6. Add the shrimp and cook for 4–5 minutes until no longer pink.
7. Remove the shrimp, peel and set aside.
8. Add the mussels to the stock and cook until they open up.
9. Remove the mussels and discard any unopened ones. Extract their meat set aside.

10. Heat a few tablespoons of oil in a medium saucepan or skillet over medium heat.
11. Fry the fish steaks until easily flaked. Drain the fish using paper towels. Shred the meat, remove the skin and bones, and set aside.
12. To the same pan, add the onion, tomatoes, garlic, and cilantro; stir-cook for 8–10 minutes until soft and fragrant.
13. Season with paprika and salt; stir-cook for 1 minute.
14. Heat the tomato mixture in a deep saucepan or cooking pot over medium heat. Turn heat to low and cover. Simmer the mixture for 35–40 minutes.
15. Mix in the mussels, shrimp, and fish; stir and add the lobster and crab meat.
16. Stir-cook for 8–10 minutes and serve warm.

***Nutrition (per serving)***
Calories 360, fat 15 g, carbs 12 g, protein 48 g, sodium 1027 mg

# Beef Stew in Clay Pot (Barreado)

*Serves 8 | Prep. time 10 minutes | Cooking time 8 hours*

**Ingredients**

2¼ pounds stewing beef, cubed
3½ ounces bacon strips
3 onions, chopped
6 cloves garlic, chopped
1 bunch chives, snipped
4 bay leaves
1⅓ cups water
1 teaspoon ground cumin
2 bananas, peeled and chopped
4 cups cassava flour or all-purpose flour
Chili sauce to serve

***Directions***
1. Add the beef and bacon to a clay pot or cast-iron casserole. Add the onions, chives, garlic, bay leaves, and cumin. Close the lid.
2. Add the flour to a mixing bowl, reserving 2 tablespoons; add water and combine well to make a flaky dough.
3. Shape the dough and press it around the pot rim to create a solid seal.
4. Set the pot over low heat and cook the mixture for 8 hours.
5. Add the remaining flour and the stew mixture to a serving dish; stir well.
6. Serve with some chili sauce or bananas.

***Nutrition (per serving)***
Calories 417, fat 11 g, carbs 56 g, protein 11 g, sodium 673 mg

# Black Bean Soup (Caldinho de Carne)

*Serves 8 | Prep. time 10–15 minutes | Cooking time 70–80 minutes*

### Ingredients
½ teaspoon Tabasco sauce (optional)
½ teaspoon cumin
2 tablespoons olive oil
2 bay leaves
¼ cup pancetta
1 pound black beans, soaked overnight and drained
2 quarts water
¼ cup parsley, chopped
1 onion, chopped
4 cloves garlic, minced
Fried pancetta or bacon to garnish

Chopped parsley or green onions to garnish

### *Directions*
1. Add the water to a pressure cooker along with the bay leaves and beans. Close the lid and pressure cook for 40–50 minutes until the beans are softened.
2. Add the pancetta to a medium saucepan or skillet and heat over medium heat until golden brown.
3. Add the oil and heat it. Add the onion and garlic; stir-cook for 5 minutes until soft and translucent.
4. Add this mixture to the bean mixture and mix in the Tabasco sauce, cumin and parsley. Simmer the mixture, uncovered, for 15–20 minutes.
5. Transfer the bean mixture to a blender and blend until smooth.
6. Season with black pepper and salt. Serve with French bread with the chopped green onions or parsley and bacon/pancetta on top.

### *Nutrition (per serving)*
Calories 246, fat 7 g, carbs 36 g, protein 13 g, sodium 369 mg

# Coconut Butternut Squash Soup (Sopa e Abobora e Coco)

*Serves 6 | Prep. time 10 minutes | Cooking time 35–40 minutes*

**Ingredients**
2 tablespoons olive oil
1 medium butternut squash, peeled and cut into 1-inch cubes
1 medium onion, peeled and diced
1 large peeled sweet potato, cut into 1-inch cubes
1 tablespoon brown sugar
1 teaspoon salt
1 teaspoon cumin
1 quart vegetable stock
¼ teaspoon red pepper flakes
1 (13½-ounce) can coconut milk

1 small bunch kale, stemmed and cut into thin ribbons
2 tablespoons lime juice
1 cup pepitas (pumpkin seeds)

### *Directions*
1. Heat the oil in a deep saucepan or cooking pot over medium heat.
2. Add the onion; stir-cook for 5–6 minutes until soft and translucent.
3. Add the sweet potato, squash, cumin, salt, brown sugar, and red pepper flakes. Stir-cook for 8–10 minutes, until the squash turns light brown.
4. Add the stock and stir.
5. Bring the mixture to boil; turn heat to low and cover. Simmer the mixture for 8–10 minutes until the potatoes are tender.
6. Take out only the vegetables and transfer them to a blender.
7. Add the lime juice and coconut milk. Blend to make a smooth mixture.
8. Add the mixture to the saucepan along with the kale; stir and simmer for 3–5 minutes more. Serve topped with the pepitas.

### *Nutrition (per serving)*
Calories 380, fat 29 g, carbs 27 g, protein 10 g, sodium 590 mg

# Cream Corn Soup
# (Creme de Milho Verde)

*Serves 4 | Prep. time 10–15 minutes | Cooking time 15 minutes*

### Ingredients
½ large white onion, chopped
2 tablespoons vegetable oil
3 cloves garlic, minced
1 large potato, peeled and cut into chunks
1½ quarts chicken or vegetable stock
3¼ cups fresh corn kernels (divided)
1½ teaspoons salt
1½ teaspoons ground black pepper
Heavy cream or yogurt to taste

*Directions*
1. Heat the oil in a medium saucepan or skillet over medium heat.
2. Add the onion; stir-cook for 3–4 minutes until soft and translucent.
3. Add the garlic and stir-cook for 1 minute until brown and fragrant.
4. Add the broth and boil the mixture.
5. Add the potatoes and 2¼ cups of the corn kernels; season with black pepper and salt.
6. Stir-cook until the potatoes are tender.
7. To a blender, add the potato mixture and yogurt or cream. Blend to make a smooth, creamy mixture.
8. Season to taste. Pour the mixture into a container and mix in the remaining corn kernels.
9. Serve warm with fresh chives and chopped cooked sausage on top (optional).

*Nutrition (per serving)*
Calories 356, fat 13 g, carbs 48 g, protein 14 g, sodium 1391 mg

# Shrimp Stew (Vatapa)

*Serves 6–8 | Prep. time 10 minutes |
Cooking time 75–80 minutes*

### Ingredients
6 ounces dried salt cod
¼ cup plain, unsalted peanuts
½ cup small dried shrimp
¼ cup cashews
3 scallions, trimmed and thinly sliced
2 dried chilies de arbol, stemmed
5 ounces white country bread, thinly sliced
1 (14-ounce) can coconut milk
2 cloves garlic
1 (1-inch) piece peeled ginger, thinly sliced crosswise
½ cup palm oil

1 small onion, finely chopped
3 canned whole peeled tomatoes, crushed by hand
½ pound raw medium shrimp, peeled and deveined
3 cups fish stock
Salt and black pepper to taste
Cooked rice to serve

### *Directions*

1. To a deep saucepan or cooking pot, add the fish and enough cold water to cover and heat over medium heat.
2. Boil the mixture for 20 minutes; drain and repeat twice more.
3. Shred the fish and set aside.
4. Add the cashews, dried shrimp, peanuts, chilies, scallions, garlic, and ginger to a blender and blend to make a smooth mixture. Remove and set aside.
5. Clean the blender and then add the coconut milk and bread to it. Set aside for 15–20 minutes and then blend to make a smooth mixture.
6. Heat the oil in a medium saucepan or skillet over medium heat.
7. Add the onion; stir-cook for 10–12 minutes until soft and translucent.
8. Mix in the shrimp paste; stir-cook for 2 minutes.
9. Add the tomatoes; stir-cook for 5–6 minutes until soft.
10. Add the bread paste, shredded fish and stock.
11. Bring the mixture to boil; turn heat to medium-low. Simmer for 25–30 minutes until the volume reduces to one-fourth.
12. Mix in the shrimp and cook for 2–3 minutes until no longer pink. Season to taste and serve with steamed rice.

### *Nutrition (per serving)*
Calories 333, fat 18 g, carbs 16 g, protein 24 g, sodium 1946 mg

# MAIN ENTRÉES

## Beef Rump Steak BBQ (Picanha with Farofa)

*Serves 4 | Prep. time 10 minutes | Cooking time 10 minutes*

**Ingredients**
Picanha
2 tablespoons Brazilian sofrito
¼ teaspoon mustard powder
2½ pounds picanha
Coarse salt to taste
½ teaspoon dried parsley
Lemon pepper or ground black pepper to taste

Farofa
½ onion, sliced
2 tablespoons fresh cilantro, chopped
1 cup cassava flour
½ cup unsalted butter
4 whole eggs
Black pepper and salt to taste

**Directions**
1. Preheat the oven or grill to 350°F.
2. In a mixing bowl, combine the dry parsley, sofrito, mustard and a drizzle of olive oil. Set aside.
3. Cut the meat into 4 steaks in the direction of the fibers. Season with pepper and salt; coat the steaks with the sofrito mixture.
4. Grill the steaks until cooked well and evenly. Let cool and slice.
5. Heat the butter in a medium saucepan or skillet over medium heat.
6. Add the onion; stir-cook for 2–3 minutes until soft and translucent.
7. Add the eggs and scramble gently. Mix in the cassava and remove from heat.
8. Mix in the cilantro. Season with black pepper and salt.
9. Serve the steaks with the cassava mixture.

**Nutrition (per serving)**
Calories 742, fat 48 g, carbs 28 g, protein 53 g, sodium 412 mg

# Brazilian BBQ (Churrasco)

*Serves 4 | Prep. time 10 minutes | Cooking time 10 minutes*

**Ingredients**
6 medium cloves garlic, minced
Salt to taste
1½ pounds skirt steak, trimmed and cut into 4 pieces
Freshly ground black pepper
2 tablespoons canola oil or vegetable oil
¼ cup unsalted butter
1 tablespoon flat-leaf parsley, chopped

**Directions**
1. Season the steak with black pepper and salt.
2. Heat the oil in a medium saucepan or skillet over medium heat.

3. Add the steak; stir-cook for 2–3 minutes to evenly brown. Set aside to cool down.
4. Melt the butter in the same pan.
5. Add the garlic; stir-cook for 3–4 minutes until fragrant. Add some salt to taste.
6. Slice the steak and add the garlic butter on top.
7. Serve topped with some parsley.

**Nutrition (per serving)**
Calories 450, fat 33 g, carbs 2 g, protein 36 g, sodium 400 mg

# Brazilian Chicken Pot Pie (Empadao de Frango)

*Serves 10 | Prep. time 40 minutes | Cooking time 50 minutes*

## *Ingredients*

Filling

2 cloves garlic, minced
2 tomatoes, chopped
2 tablespoons olive oil
2 medium onions, finely chopped
2 pounds chicken breast, cooked and shredded
1 cup hearts of palm, chopped (optional)
½ cup green olives, chopped
1 cup corn (optional)
1 cup green peas (optional)
1 cup tomato sauce
1 tablespoon all-purpose flour mixed with ⅓ cup milk
½ cup parsley, chopped
1–2 dashes hot sauce
2 cups chicken broth
Ground black pepper and salt to taste

Crust

3 egg yolks
¼–½ cup cold water
5 cups flour
1 teaspoon salt
1 egg yolk, lightly beaten, for brushing
1½ cups butter, cut into small pieces

## *Directions*

Filling

1. Heat the oil in a medium saucepan or skillet over medium heat.
2. Add the onion; stir-cook until soft and translucent.
3. Add the garlic and stir-cook until brown and fragrant.
4. Add the tomatoes; stir-cook for 2–3 minutes until softened.
5. Mix in the peas, corn, chicken, olives, hot sauce, tomato sauce, and palm hearts.
6. Add the broth and flour mixture; combine well.

7. Turn heat to low. Simmer the mixture while stirring for 8–10 minutes until thickened.
8. Mix in the chopped parsley; season with black pepper and salt to taste.
9. Let cool.

Crust
1. Combine the salt and flour in a mixing bowl.
2. Beat the eggs and mix with the flour mixture; add the butter and combine until finely crumbed.
3. Add a few tablespoons of water in batches and keep mixing to prepare a flaky dough.
4. Cover the dough and refrigerate for 20–30 minutes.
5. Preheat the oven to 350°F.
6. Roll ⅔ of the dough into a large round of about 12 inches.
7. Add the dough to a 9-inch pastry pan, covering the sides of the pan as well as the bottom. Prick the dough using a fork.
8. Add the prepared filling and distribute it evenly.
9. Roll the remaining dough into a round shape that fits the top of the pan.
10. Place it over the pan and crimp the edges to make a seal.
11. Make two cuts on top to let steam escape. Gently brush the pie with the egg yolk.
12. Bake for 20–25 minutes until the edges turn golden brown.
13. Slice and serve warm.

***Nutrition (per serving)***
Calories 628, fat 17 g, carbs 62 g, protein 42 g, sodium 737 mg

# Roasted Pork Loin (Lombo Assado)

*Serves 4–6 | Prep. time 20–30 minutes | Cooking time 2 hours 10 minutes*

### Ingredients
1 (3-pound) boneless center-cut pork loin, rinsed and dried
1 cup orange juice
2 cloves garlic, chopped
1 bay leaf, crushed
1 lime
1 medium yellow onion, chopped
1 small bunch flat-leaf parsley
1 teaspoon salt
8 black peppercorns
½ cup green onions, chopped
Brazilian rice to serve (optional)

*Directions*
1. Add the orange juice, bay leaf, garlic, and onions to a blender and blend to make a smooth mixture.
2. Take 8 to 10 sprigs of parsley from the small bunch, wrap them and refrigerate.
3. Chop the leaves from the remaining parsley, remove the stems, and add them to the blender. Add the black pepper and salt. Blend to make a smooth marinade mixture.
4. Coat the pork with the marinade mixture in a bowl; cover and refrigerate for 5–6 hours or overnight.
5. Preheat the oven to 375°F. Grease a roasting pan with some vegetable oil.
6. Remove the pork from the marinade, reserving the marinade, and place it in the pan.
7. Roast the pork on the middle rack for about 25 minutes.
8. Add ⅓ of the marinade over the pork and continue roasting for 1½ hours, basting the meat every 30–40 minutes. Reserve the pan drippings.
9. Roast until the pork is well cooked and tender.
10. Chop the refrigerated parsley and set aside.
11. Heat the drippings in a medium saucepan or skillet over medium heat.
12. Add the green onions and parsley; stir-cook for 1–2 minutes until soft and translucent.
13. Slice the pork and add the onion mixture on top. Serve with cooked Brazilian rice.

*Nutrition (per serving)*
Calories 154, fat 4 g, carbs 14 g, protein 14 g, sodium 443 mg

# Brazilian Marinated Chicken

*Serves 4 | Prep. time 15–20 minutes | Cooking time 60–70 minutes*

***Ingredients***
5 sage leaves, finely chopped
2 tablespoons cachaca (Brazillian spirit)
1 tablespoon soft brown sugar
1 medium (3-pound) chicken
Olive oil for drizzling
Sea salt and black pepper to taste

Marinade
3 tablespoons cachaca
Juice of 2 large limes
3 cloves garlic, finely chopped or crushed
2 tablespoons soft brown sugar
½ teaspoon sea salt

5–6 large sage leaves, finely chopped
2 tablespoons olive or rapeseed oil

### *Directions*
1. Preheat the oven to 400°F.
2. Coat the chicken with olive oil. Season with the sage, salt, and black pepper.
3. Add all the marinade ingredients to a mixing bowl and stir to dissolve the sugar.
4. Grease a large roasting pan with some vegetable oil. Add the marinade to the pan along with the chicken. Cover the chicken neck cavity with a piece of foil.
5. Wrap the pan with foil and roast for 45–55 minutes until cooked well.
6. Combine the sugar and remaining cachaca in a bowl. Brush it over the chicken; roast for 10–15 more minutes until juices run clear and chicken is golden brown.
7. Cool down and serve drizzled with the marinade.

### *Nutrition (per serving)*
Calories 488, fat 16 g, carbs 18 g, protein 63 g, sodium 553 mg

# Grilled Chicken Leg Wrapped in Bacon
# (Churrasco de Frango com Bacon)

*Serves 6 | Prep. time 10–15 minutes | Cooking time 15 minutes*

**Ingredients**
2¼ cups olive oil (not extra-virgin)
4½ pounds chicken drumsticks, skinned
4½ cups brown ale or beer
2 tablespoons salt
2 teaspoons black pepper
8 cloves garlic, minced
1 tablespoon garlic powder
2 teaspoons onion powder
1 tablespoon dark brown sugar, packed
2 bay leaves

2 tablespoons fresh Italian oregano, chopped
1 pound smoked bacon, thick cut

### *Directions*
1. Add all the ingredients except the bacon to a mixing bowl; combine well.
2. Divide the mixture between two Ziploc bags. Seal the bags and refrigerate for 2–4 hours or overnight, flipping after 2–3 hours.
3. Remove the drumsticks and arrange over a baking sheet, reserving the marinade.
4. Wrap the bacon around each drumstick. You can use the skewers to thread the drumsticks and then grill them, or you can place them directly on the grill.
5. Preheat your grill over medium heat and grease it with some cooking spray.
6. Place the drumsticks on the grill and baste them with the reserved marinade.
7. Grill the drumsticks, turning occasionally, until evenly brown and cooked to your satisfaction.
8. Serve with grilled corn or your choice of salad.

### *Nutrition (per serving)*
Calories 853, fat 47 g, carbs 22 g, protein 52 g, sodium 2354 mg

# Ground Beef Kebab (Kafta no Espeto)

*Serves 12 | Prep. time 15–20 minutes | Cooking time 15–20 minutes*

### Ingredients
2 cloves garlic, crushed
2 teaspoons salt (divided)
1 cup plain Greek yogurt
2 pounds ground beef
½ cup tahini
3 tablespoons lime juice

2 teaspoons ground black pepper (divided)
1 teaspoon + 2 tablespoons parsley, minced (divided)
4 slices bacon, finely chopped
1 small onion, peeled and grated
2 cloves garlic, finely minced
1 teaspoon ground cumin
2 tablespoons parsley, minced
1 tablespoon mint, minced
1 teaspoon smoked paprika
½ teaspoon ground cinnamon

### *Directions*
1. Preheat your grill. Soak wooden skewers in water for 30–40 minutes.
2. Whisk the tahini and yogurt in a mixing bowl.
3. Crush the garlic with 1 teaspoon of the salt. Add it to the bowl and combine.
4. Mix in the lemon juice, 1 teaspoon of the black pepper, and 1 tablespoon of the parsley; set aside.
5. In another bowl, combine the bacon, ground beef, onion, mint, garlic, cinnamon, cumin, paprika and the remaining salt, black pepper, and parsley.
6. Prepare sausages from the mixture and thread onto the skewers.
7. Grill for 3–4 minutes per side until cooked well and evenly browned.
8. Serve with the yogurt mixture.

### *Nutrition (per serving)*
Calories 280, fat 21 g, carbs 5 g, protein 19 g, sodium 1510 mg

*THIS ONE IS EXTRA TASTY?!*

# Bahian Style Coconut Chicken (Moqueca de Frango)

*Serves 4 | Prep. time 10–15 minutes | Cooking time 40 minutes*

### Ingredients
2 large onions, sliced thick
1 green bell pepper, sliced thick
1 red bell pepper, sliced thick
3-4 boneless chicken breasts, cubed
Black pepper to taste
3 tomatoes, skinned, seeded and chopped
1 red pepper, chopped
1 cube chicken broth
1 tablespoon olive oil or palm oil
Juice of 1 lemon juice
1 tablespoon vegetable oil

1 cup coconut milk
2 tablespoons parsley, chopped
1 teaspoon coriander, chopped

**Directions**
1. Season the chicken pieces with a little pepper, salt, and lemon juice. Set aside to marinade for 10–15 minutes.
2. Heat the vegetable oil in a medium saucepan or skillet over medium heat.
3. Add the chicken pieces; stir-cook to evenly brown.
4. Add the onion and peppers; stir-cook until soft and translucent.
5. Add the tomatoes and black pepper; stir-cook for 1 minute.
6. Mix in 1 cup of boiling water and the broth cube; stir until dissolved well.
7. Turn heat to low and cover. Simmer the mixture for 35–40 minutes until the chicken is tender.
8. Mix in the coconut milk, coriander, parsley, and palm oil; heat the mixture for a while.
9. Serve warm with cooked rice.

**Nutrition (per serving)**
Calories 280, fat 11 g, carbs 14 g, protein 7 g, sodium 282 mg

# Baked Salt Cod with Onions, Peppers, and Potatoes (Bacalhau Ao Forno)

*Serves 4-6 | Prep. time 10–15 minutes | Cooking time 60 minutes*

### Ingredients
4–5 cloves garlic, chopped
4 salted cod fish fillets (½ inch thick), soaked and dried, cut into chunks
2–3 medium tomatoes, boiled, peeled and sliced
2 medium onions, chopped

2 red peppers, trimmed and cut into strips
½ cup white wine
⅓ cup olive oil
4½ cups potatoes, quartered
1 bay leaf
¼ cup olive oil
1 tablespoon chopped fresh herbs such as parsley and chives (optional)

### Directions
1. Add half of the wine and half of the olive oil to a medium-size rectangular casserole dish.
2. Add the onions, tomatoes, and garlic; then add the potatoes and bay leaf.
3. Place the fish on top and add the remaining olive oil and wine.
4. Preheat the oven to 380°F.
5. Bake for 55–60 minutes, basting the fish periodically with the cooking juices until the fish and potatoes are cooked well.
6. Remove bay leaf and serve topped with some herbs, if desired.

### Nutrition (per serving)
Calories 582, fat 31 g, carbs 43 g, protein 9 g, sodium 259 mg

# Fish Baked in Banana Leaves
# (Peixena Folha de Bananeira)

*Serves 6 | Prep. time 10 minutes | Cooking time 25 minutes*

### Ingredients
¼ cup coconut milk
1 small red chili pepper, seeded
3 tablespoons lime juice
1 teaspoon salt
1 teaspoon ground black pepper
¼ cup fresh cilantro, chopped
4 large (6 ounces each) cod fillets
4 large banana leaves

### Directions
1. Add the cilantro, coconut milk, black pepper, lime juice, salt, and chili pepper to a blender and blend to make a smooth mixture.

2. Place the marinade and fish in a baking dish. Refrigerate for 30–45 minutes.
3. Preheat the oven to 375°F.
4. Place each fish fillet over a banana leaf. Top with 1–2 tablespoons of the marinade and seal the edges with a toothpick or twine.
5. Place the sealed packets over a baking sheet.
6. Bake for 20–25 minutes until the fish is easy to flake.
7. Serve warm.

**Nutrition (per serving)**
Calories 110, fat 2.5 g, carbs 2 g, protein 18 g, sodium 450 mg

# Shrimp Bobo (Bobo de Camarao)

*Serves 8 | Prep. time 10 minutes | Cooking time 20 minutes*

### Ingredients
Cream
2 green bell peppers, seeded and chopped
¼ cup cilantro, finely chopped
2 pounds onions, peeled and chopped
2 pounds firm, ripe tomatoes, seeded and chopped
2 pounds manioc/cassava/yuca root, peeled, boiled and mashed
1 quart coconut milk
2 cups extra-virgin olive oil

Shrimp
2 tablespoons cilantro, finely chopped
3 medium tomatoes, seeded and chopped

3 medium onions, chopped
1 clove garlic, minced
4 pounds medium or large shrimp, peeled and deveined
1 tablespoons salt
1 quart coconut milk
1 green bell pepper, seeded and chopped
½ cup extra-virgin olive oil
2 tablespoons dende (palm) oil

### Directions

1. Heat the olive oil in a medium saucepan or skillet over medium heat.
2. Add the manioc, tomatoes, onion, green pepper and cilantro.
3. Mix in the coconut milk; stir-cook for 10–12 minutes.
4. Remove from heat and set aside.
5. Rinse and drain the shrimp.
6. Heat the olive oil in a deep saucepan or cooking pot over medium heat.
7. Add the shrimp, salt, garlic, tomatoes, cilantro, onions and green pepper; stir-cook for 1–2 minutes.
8. Add the coconut milk and stir-cook for 4–5 more minutes.
9. Mix in the manioc mixture and stir-cook for 4–5 more minutes.
10. Mix in the dende oil.
11. Serve topped with some cilantro.

### Nutrition (per serving)
Calories 713, fat 28 g, carbs 61 g, protein 51 g, sodium 1874 mg

# Chicken Skewers with Pineapple and Bacon
# (Espetinho de Frango com Bacon)

*Serves 2–4 | Prep. time 15–20 minutes | Cooking time 20–30 minutes*

### Ingredients
1½ cups BBQ sauce
Fresh pineapple, cut into 2-inch chunks
2 large chicken breasts, cut into 1½–2-inch chunks, salted lightly
1 pound bacon, cut into 1–1½-inch segments

### Directions
1. Combine the chicken pieces and half the BBQ sauce in a bowl. Set aside to marinate for 2–3 hours.
2. Heat the bacon in the microwave for 2–3 minutes until almost crispy. Let cool.
3. Thread the chicken onto skewers, then thread the bacon and pineapple. Repeat, keeping some space in between.
4. Preheat your grill to 155–160°F.
5. Place the skewers to grill.
6. Drizzle the remaining BBQ sauce over the skewers when the chicken is nearly cooked.
7. Set aside for 5–10 minutes and serve warm.

### Nutrition (per serving)
Calories 520, fat 40 g, carbs 22 g, protein 51 g, sodium 1741 mg

# Bahian Seafood Stew
# (Mequeca de Peixe Baiana)

*Serves 4 | Prep. time 10 minutes | Cooking time 35 minutes*

**Ingredients**
Soup
1½–2 pounds fillets of firm white fish (halibut, swordfish, or cod)
Ground black pepper and salt to taste
2 tablespoons olive oil
3 cloves garlic, minced
¼ cup lime or lemon juice
½ yellow and ½ red bell pepper, seeded, de-stemmed, and chopped or sliced
2 cups tomatoes, chopped or sliced
1 cup spring onion, chopped or sliced
¼ cup green onion greens, chopped
1 tablespoon paprika

Pinch red pepper flakes
1 (14-ounce) can coconut milk
1 large bunch cilantro, chopped

Rice
1 clove garlic, minced
1 cup white rice
1 tablespoon olive oil
½ onion, chopped
1¾ cups boiling water
1 teaspoon salt

***Directions***
1. Rinse the fish in cold water; remove the bones and chop into large pieces.
2. Toss the fish pieces with lime juice and garlic in a bowl. Season with black pepper and salt. Place in the refrigerator.

Rice
1. Heat the olive oil in a medium saucepan or skillet over medium heat.
2. Add the onion; stir-cook until soft and translucent.
3. Add the garlic and stir-cook for 30 seconds until brown and fragrant.
4. Add the rice and combine well. Pour in the boiling water and add the salt.
5. Turn heat to low and cover. Simmer for 15 minutes.
6. Set aside to cool.

Soup
1. Heat the olive oil in a deep saucepan or cooking pot over medium heat.
2. Add the onion; stir-cook until soft and translucent.
3. Add the bell pepper, pepper flakes and paprika; season with black pepper and salt. Stir-cook until the bell pepper is softened.

4. Add the green onions and tomatoes; stir and simmer the mixture for 4–5 minutes.
5. Add the cilantro and stir.
6. Remove half of the vegetables; add the fish pieces and season with black pepper and salt.
7. Return the removed vegetables on top; mix in the coconut milk.
8. Turn heat to low and cover. Simmer for 15 minutes.
9. Add more seasoning or lemon juice if required.
10. Serve topped with cilantro and cooked rice or bread of your choice.

*Nutrition (per serving)*
Calories 356, fat 10 g, carbs 51 g, protein 13 g, sodium 659 mg

# Crazy Beef Sandwich (Sanduiche de Carne Louca)

*Serves 20 | Prep. time 30 minutes | Cooking time 2 hours*

### Ingredients
2 pounds beef chuck (cut into 2-inch cubes)
1 tablespoon soy sauce
1 tablespoon coarse spicy mustard
¼ cup vegetable oil
¼ cup red wine vinegar
2 cloves garlic, minced
1 teaspoon Worcestershire sauce
1 medium onion, sliced
1 medium onion, diced
1 green bell pepper, cut into strips
1 teaspoon oregano
1 tomato, seeded and diced
2 tablespoons tomato paste
1–2 cups beef stock
1 tablespoon cornstarch
2 tablespoons cachaca, rum, or water
1 tablespoon chili pepper paste or ½ teaspoon hot pepper sauce (optional)
1 tablespoon capers
¼ cup green onions, chopped
Sandwich rolls to serve
Sliced cheese (optional)

### Directions
1. Combine the vinegar, vegetable oil, soy sauce and mustard in a mixing bowl.
2. Add the beef and mix.
3. Cover and refrigerate for 6–8 hours or overnight.
4. Add the beef to a medium saucepan or skillet over medium heat; stir-cook to brown evenly. Set aside.
5. Add the diced onions and beef marinade to the same pan. Stir-cook until softened.
6. Add the tomatoes and garlic; stir-cook until softened.

7. Mix in the sliced onions, tomato paste, green pepper, and oregano; stir-cook for 1–2 minutes more.
8. Add the browned beef and enough water to cover.
9. Turn heat to low and cover. Simmer the mixture for 1–2 hours, until the meat is tender and easy to shred.
10. Combine the cornstarch, cachaca and chili pepper paste/hot sauce in a mixing bowl. Make sure to dissolve the cornstarch.
11. Add the mixture to the pan and cook until it thickens.
12. Mix in the green onions and capers.
13. Let cool.
14. Arrange between the sandwich rolls, add cheese if desired, and serve.

***Nutrition (per serving)***
Calories 138, fat 10 g, carbs 4 g, protein 9 g, sodium 136 mg

# VEGETARIAN, SIDES, BEANS AND RICE

## Vegetarian Bobo (Bobo Vegetariano)

*Serves 6–8 | Prep. time 10 minutes | Cooking time 65–70 minutes*

**Ingredients**
- 1 large white onion, finely sliced
- 1 pound peeled yuca root, chopped into small pieces
- 3 cups vegetable broth
- 2 tablespoons olive oil
- 1 green bell pepper, seeded and finely sliced

1 red bell pepper, seeded and finely sliced
3 big red tomatoes, chopped
2 large cloves garlic, minced
1 (14-ounce) can coconut milk
1 teaspoon paprika
1 cup cilantro, chopped
1 tablespoon dried red chili peppers, crushed
Black pepper and salt to taste

**Directions**
1. Heat the broth in a medium saucepan or skillet over medium heat.
2. Add the yuca root; boil for 40–45 minutes to soften.
3. Transfer the yuca to a blender along with the broth. Blend to make a smooth mixture.
4. Heat the oil in a medium saucepan or skillet over medium heat.
5. Add the onion, garlic, and peppers; stir-cook for 4–5 minutes to soften.
6. Add the tomatoes. Cover and cook for 6–7 minutes until the vegetables are softened.
7. Mix in the red pepper flakes, paprika, coconut milk and yuca mixture; stir-cook for 2–3 minutes.
8. Season to taste, top with the cilantro and serve.

**Nutrition (per serving)**
Calories 263, fat 12 g, carbs 36 g, protein 2 g, sodium 229 mg

# Heart of Palm Bahian Stew
# (Moqueca de Palmito)

*Serves 4 | Prep. time 15 minutes | Cooking time 20 minutes*

**Ingredients**
½ large onion, sliced
½ green bell pepper, sliced into rings
½ red bell pepper, sliced into rings
3 teaspoons palm oil (divided)
½ tablespoon olive oil
1 large tomato, chopped
1 (14-ounce) can coconut milk
1 (15-ounce) can heart of palm, drained and sliced
Salt to taste

2 tablespoons parsley, chopped, or to taste

### *Directions*
1. Heat the olive oil and 1 teaspoon of the palm oil in a medium saucepan or skillet over medium heat.
2. Add the onion; stir-cook for 4–5 minutes until soft and translucent.
3. Add the bell peppers; stir-cook for 2–3 minutes.
4. Mix in the palm hearts, tomato, and remaining palm oil; stir the mixture.
5. Mix in the coconut milk and season with some salt.
6. Add the parsley and simmer for 9–10 minutes until the mixture turns soft.
7. Serve warm.

### *Nutrition (per serving)*
Calories 292, fat 27 g, carbs 13 g, protein 6 g, sodium 510 mg

# Farofa with Plantains
# (Farofa de Banana)

*Serves 4 | Prep. time 5 minutes | Cooking time 10 minutes*

**Ingredients**
2 tablespoons butter
1 onion, finely chopped
3 plantains or bananas, peeled and sliced
Oil to fry
Pinch of sugar
1 cup cassava flour
Salt to taste
Chopped spring onion to serve

*Directions*
1. Heat some oil in a medium saucepan or skillet over medium heat.
2. Add the plantains; stir-cook for 2–3 minutes until golden brown. Set aside.
3. In the same pan, melt the butter and sauté the onions for 3–4 minutes until softened.
4. Add the sugar and cooked plantains; top with the flour and stir the mixture. Season with some salt.
5. Stir-cook for 2–3 minutes and allow it to cool.
6. Top with the spring onions and serve warm.

*Nutrition (per serving)*
Calories 334, fat 6 g, carbs 41 g, protein 4 g, sodium 202 mg

# Farofa with Fried Bacon

*Serves 4 | Prep. time 5 minutes | Cooking time 5 minutes*

**Ingredients**

5 slices bacon, finely diced
2 cups toasted manioc flour
2 tablespoons vegetable oil

**Directions**

1. Heat the oil in a medium saucepan or skillet over medium heat.
2. Add the bacon; stir-cook until crisp and brown.
3. Remove from heat and add the flour. Combine well until the flour absorbs the oil.
4. Serve warm.

***Nutrition (per serving)***
Calories 237, fat 12 g, carbs 46 g, protein 6 g, sodium 340 mg

# Everyday Black Beans (Feijao Preto)

*Serves 8–10 | Prep. time 10 minutes | Cooking time 55–60 minutes*

**Ingredients**
1 pound dry black beans
Black pepper and salt to taste
14 ounces smoked sausage, cut into chunks
1 bay leaf
½ teaspoon white vinegar

½ teaspoon cumin
4 strips smoked bacon, cut into lardons
1 medium onion, diced
6 cloves garlic, minced
2 tablespoons olive oil

*Directions*
1. Add the beans and enough cold water to cover to a large or medium size bowl. Allow soaking for 30 minutes.
2. Drain the water, add fresh cold water, and soak for 30 more minutes.
3. Drain the water and transfer the beans to a pressure cooker or Instant Pot.
4. Add 5 cups of water and the sausage. Close the lid and pressure cook for 30 minutes.
5. Open the lid and stir-cook the beans over medium-low heat.
6. Season with black pepper and salt.
7. Mix in the vinegar, cumin and bay leaf. Stir and simmer for 15 minutes. Set aside.
8. Add the bacon to a medium saucepan or skillet and stir-cook over medium heat until crisp and evenly brown.
9. Add and heat the oil. Add the onion; stir-cook for 2–3 minutes until soft and translucent.
10. Add the garlic and stir-cook until fragrant.
11. Add the mixture with the beans. Stir-cook until it thickens to your satisfaction.
12. Serve warm.

*Nutrition (per serving)*
Calories 153, fat 6 g, carbs 17 g, protein 9 g, sodium 171 mg

# Coconut Beans (Feijao de Coco)

*Serves 6–8 | Prep. time 10 minutes | Cooking time 25–30 minutes*

### Ingredients
1 teaspoon ground cumin
3 cloves garlic, crushed or chopped
1 tablespoon fresh coriander, chopped
Salt and ground black pepper to taste
1 large onion, chopped
2 cups black-eyed peas
2 bay leaves
7 ounces coconut milk

### Directions
1. Add the black-eyed peas to a pressure cooker with enough water to cover.
2. Add the cumin, black pepper, bay leaves, and salt.
3. Stir the mixture, close the lid, and pressure cook for 15 minutes.
4. Open the lid and add the coriander, garlic, and onions; stir-cook for 8–10 minutes until the black-eyed peas are cooked well. Allow cooling for 10 minutes.
5. Add ⅓ of the mixture and ⅓ of the coconut milk to a blender.
6. Blend to make a smooth mixture. Strain and set aside.
7. Repeat with the remaining thirds.
8. Serve warm.

### Nutrition (per serving)
Calories 98, fat 5 g, carbs 10 g, protein 4 g, sodium 216 mg

# Black Beans and Rice (Feijao de Feijao Preto)

*Serves 4–6 | Prep. time 8–10 minutes | Cooking time 30–40 minutes*

### *Ingredients*
Rice
1 cup long-grain white rice, washed and drained
2 tablespoons vegetable oil
1 tablespoon onion, finely chopped
2 cups cold water (divided)
1 teaspoon salt

Beans
1 clove garlic, finely chopped
1 (16-ounce) can black beans or pinto beans in brine, rinsed and drained
1 tablespoon vegetable oil
1 tablespoon diced bacon (optional)
1 cup water
Salt to taste
1 teaspoon green onion or chives, finely chopped

### *Directions*
Rice
1. Heat the oil in a medium saucepan or skillet over medium heat.
2. Add the onion; stir-cook until soft and translucent.
3. Add the rice and stir-cook until chalky and whitish.
4. Add 1½ cups of the water and the salt.
5. Bring the mixture to boil. Turn heat to low and partially cover the pan. Simmer until the liquid evaporates.
6. Add the remaining water and cook until the liquid evaporates and the rice grains are cooked well.
7. Set aside to cool down; fluff the mixture and serve.

Beans
1. In a medium saucepan or skillet over medium heat, stir-cook the bacon until crisp and evenly brown.
2. Add the garlic and cook until fragrant.
3. Turn heat to low, add the beans and gently mash them.
4. Add the water. Boil the mixture and cook until brown colored and thickened.
5. Season with salt. Serve with the chives or green onions on top.

*Nutrition (per serving)*
Calories 177, fat 8 g, carbs 23 g, protein 6 g, sodium 634 mg

# Rice, Beans, and Sausages (Feijao Com Linguica)

*Serves 6 | Prep. time 5 minutes | Cooking time 35 minutes*

### Ingredients
½ cup green onion, chopped
3 cloves garlic, minced
2 tablespoons oil
1 pound smoked sausage, sliced
1 cup rice, uncooked
14 ounces pinto beans, drained and rinsed
2 cups chicken broth
Black pepper and salt to taste
1–2 bay leaves

### Directions
1. Heat the oil in a medium saucepan or skillet over medium heat.
2. Add the green onion, sausage, and garlic; stir-cook until the onions turn soft and translucent.
3. Mix in the rice and remaining ingredients.
4. Bring the mixture to boil; turn heat to low and cover. Simmer for 20–25 minutes until the rice is cooked well.
5. Fluff and serve.

### Nutrition (per serving)
Calories 395, fat 25 g, carbs 24 g, protein 14 g, sodium 912 mg

# Brazilian Rice (Arroz Brasileiro)

*Serves 4 | Prep. time 8–10 minutes |
Cooking time 25–30 minutes*

### Ingredients
1 small onion, finely chopped
2 cloves garlic, finely chopped
1 cup basmati or jasmine rice, washed and drained
1½ tablespoons olive oil
1 teaspoon salt
2 cups boiling water

### Directions
1. Heat the oil in a medium saucepan or skillet over medium heat.
2. Add in the garlic and onion; stir-cook for 3–4 minutes until soft and translucent.
3. Add the rice and stir-cook for 3–4 minutes.

4. Add the boiling water and salt; stir to combine.
5. Cover and cook for about 8 minutes.
6. Turn heat to low and cover. Simmer the mixture until the liquid evaporates.
7. Serve warm.

***Nutrition (per serving)***
Calories 207, fat 7 g, carbs 36 g, protein 4 g, sodium 582 mg

# Black Eye Peas and Rice (Baiao de Dois)

*Serves 8–10 | Prep. time 5 minutes | Cooking time 70–80 minutes*

**Ingredients**
5 ounces chorizo, finely chopped
2 tablespoons olive oil
½ pound bacon, finely chopped
1 large yellow onion
2 teaspoons ground annatto seed
6 cloves garlic, minced
Salt and ground black pepper to taste
2½ cups jasmine rice, rinsed
1 pound dried black-eyed peas, soaked overnight and drained

*Directions*
1. Heat the oil in a medium saucepan or skillet over medium heat.
2. Add the bacon and chorizo; stir-cook for 10–12 minutes until evenly brown and fat is rendered.
3. Add the onion; stir-cook for 5–6 minutes until soft and translucent.
4. Add the garlic and stir-cook for 8–9 minutes until brown and fragrant.
5. Season with salt and black pepper and add the annatto; stir-cook for 1 minute.
6. Add 5½ cups water and the black-eyed peas.
7. Bring the mixture to boil; turn heat to low and partially cover. Simmer for 30 minutes until the black-eyed peas are tender.
8. Mix in the rice; continue to simmer for 15 minutes until the rice is cooked well.
9. Serve warm.

*Nutrition (per serving)*
Calories 366, fat 15 g, carbs 38 g, protein 22 g, sodium 669 mg

# DESSERTS

## Chocolate Truffles (Brigadeiros)

*Serves 2–4 | Prep. time 15–20 minutes | Cooking time 10–15 minutes*

*Ingredients*
1 tablespoon butter, melted
1 (14-ounce) can sweetened condensed milk
3 tablespoons cocoa powder
1 cup chocolate sprinkles
Butter, melted, to grease

*Directions*
1. Grease a serving plate with some butter.
2. Add the cocoa powder, milk and butter to a saucepan.

3. Combine and stir-cook over medium-low heat for 8–10 minutes.
4. Transfer the mixture to a serving plate and let cool.
5. Add the chocolate sprinkles to a bowl.
6. Grease your hands with some butter and prepare small balls from the cocoa mixture.
7. Roll them one by one in the bowl to cover with the sprinkles.
8. Serve.

***Nutrition (per serving)***
Calories 419, fat 17 g, carbs 63 g, protein 7 g, sodium 158 mg

# Grilled Spiced Pineapple (Abacaxi Grelhado)

*Serves 6–8 | Prep. time 5 minutes | Cooking time 40 minutes*

### Ingredients
1 tablespoon brown sugar
1 tablespoon cachaca or dark rum
1 tablespoon ground cinnamon
1 small pineapple, peeled and sliced into 6–8 thick rounds
Vanilla ice-cream to serve (optional)
Honey (optional)

### Directions
1. Top the pineapple rounds with the cachaca and cinnamon.
2. Preheat your BBQ grill.

3. Grill the rounds for 18–20 minutes to caramelize. Turn and grill for 18–20 more minutes.
4. Serve warm with the ice cream on top. Drizzle with honey if desired

***Nutrition (per serving)***
Calories 92, fat 1 g, carbs 15 g, protein 2 g, sodium 25 mg

## Coconut Custard (Quindim)

*Serves 2-4 | Prep. time 25 minutes |
Cooking time 40 minutes*

**Ingredients**
3 tablespoons butter, melted
2 teaspoons lemon or lime juice
8 egg yolks, sieved
¾ cup sugar
½ cup coconut milk
1 cup unsweetened shredded coconut
Sugar and unsalted butter (to grease and add at the bottom)

**Directions**
1. Add the coconut and milk to a mixing bowl; combine and set aside for 15 minutes.

2. Add the egg yolks and sugar to another mixing bowl. Whisk well until peaks form.
3. Mix in the lemon juice and butter. Add the coconut mixture and combine.
4. Preheat the oven to 350°F. Grease ramekins evenly with some butter and sprinkle the sugar at the bottom and edges.
5. Add the mixture to the ramekins and set aside for 10 minutes.
6. Place them in a baking dish and add hot water to cover their bottoms.
7. Bake for 30–40 minutes, until the tops turn golden brown.
8. Serve warm.

**Nutrition (per serving)**
Calories 662, fat 42 g, carbs 39 g, protein 5 g, sodium 84 mg

# Brazilian-Style Churros

*Serves 12 | Prep. time 5 minutes | Cooking time 5 minutes*

### Ingredients
1 cup flour
½ cup unsalted butter, chopped
1 tablespoon caster sugar
1½ cups water
Pinch fine salt
3½ ounces ricotta
, egg yolks
Vegetable oil for frying
1 cup canned caramel filling
½ cup cinnamon sugar

*Directions*
1. Heat the butter in a medium saucepan or skillet over medium heat.
2. Add the sugar, water, and salt; stir the mixture and cook until the sugar dissolves.
3. Add the flour and cook until the mixture starts separating from the sides.
4. Mix in the yolks and ricotta; stir the mixture well.
5. Let cool and add to a piping bag with nozzle. Chill in the refrigerator for 1 hour.
6. Heat the oil in a large frying pan or deep skillet over medium heat.
7. Squeeze the bag to make a 5-inch long churro in the heated oil.
8. Repeat to make more churros, but do not overcrowd the pan. Stir-fry until evenly brown and crisp.
9. Drain the churros on a paper towel and sprinkle with sugar.
10. Add the caramel filling to the bag.
11. Split the churros in halves and squeeze in the caramel filling. Serve warm.

*Nutrition (per serving)*
Calories 424, fat 22 g, carbs 51 g, protein 9 g, sodium 564 mg

# Coconut Tapioca Pudding
# (Cuscuz de Tapioca)

*Serves 10 | Prep. time 20 minutes | Cooking time 80–90 minutes*

**Ingredients**

1 cup unsweetened dried coconut
2 teaspoons vanilla paste or vanilla extract
1 (13-ounce) can coconut milk
2 (14-ounce) cans sweetened condensed milk
2–3 cups full fat milk
2 cups small tapioca pearls
Pinch salt
5 eggs

Caramel
½ cup water
2 cups sugar

*Directions*
1. Preheat the oven to 350°F.
2. Add the condensed milk, eggs and vanilla to a blender and blend to make a smooth mixture.
3. Add the coconut milk, full fat milk, salt and coconut to a medium saucepan or skillet; heat the mixture over medium heat.
4. Boil the mixture and remove from heat. Mix in the tapioca and set aside to cool.
5. In a medium saucepan or skillet over medium heat, heat the sugar and water to make the caramel mixture.
6. Bring the mixture to boil; turn heat to low and cover. Simmer until copper colored, taking care not to burn the sugar.
7. Add the mixture to a Bundt pan and coat the inside surface.
8. Add half the egg mixture to the tapioca mixture; stir to break up the lumps.
9. Mix in the remaining egg mixture and add to the Bundt pan.
10. Place the Bundt pan in a roasting pan; pour boiling water to cover more than halfway up the sides of the roasting pan. Bake for 60–75 minutes until the mixture jiggles in the center.
11. Cool for 45 minutes and remove the pudding. Refrigerate for 2–4 hours and serve chilled.

*Nutrition (per serving)*
Calories 486, fat 12 g, carbs 52 g, protein 11 g, sodium 421 mg

# Coconut Sweet (Queijadinha)

*Yields 11-12 | Prep. time 10 minutes | Cooking time 25 minutes*

**Ingredients**
1 (14-ounce) can sweetened condensed milk
2 eggs, lightly beaten
1 cup shredded coconut flakes
¼ cup parmesan cheese, grated or shredded

**Directions**
1. Preheat the oven to 350°F. Line 11–12 muffin cups or dessert cups with baking liners.
2. Beat the eggs in a mixing bowl. Mix in the coconut flakes, cheese, and milk; combine well.

3. Fill each muffin cup with ¼ cup of the mixture (reserve some space at the top of the cups; do not fill them completely).
4. Bake for about 25 minutes until the tops turn golden brown.
5. Serve warm.

***Nutrition (per serving)***
Calories 148, fat 7 g, carbs 19 g, protein 4 g, sodium 95 mg

# Passion Fruit Mousse
# (Mousse de Maracuja)

*Serves 8 | Prep. time 10 minutes | Cooking time 0 minutes*

**Ingredients**
1 (14-ounce) can sweetened condensed milk
1¼ cups passion fruit pulp
1 quart heavy cream
Garnishings such as chocolate shavings, cocoa nibs, toasted coconut, or toasted chopped cashews

**Directions**
1. Blend the cream in a blender until smooth.
2. Whisk the milk and passion fruit pulp in a mixing bowl.
3. Add the cream and combine well.
4. Transfer the mixture to mousse glasses.

5. Chill in the refrigerator for 2–4 hours or more if time permits.
6. Serve chilled topped with garnishes.

***Nutrition (per serving)***
Calories 449, fat 27 g, carbs 43 g, protein 7 g, sodium 86 mg

# RECIPE INDEX

**APPETIZERS AND SALADS**     **7**
Salt Cod Croquettes ........................................................... 7
(Bolinho de Balcalhau) ...................................................... 7
Cornmeal Empanadas ...................................................... 9
(Pastel de Milho) ............................................................... 9
Bahian Style Breaded Shrimp (Camarao Empanado) .... 11
Cheese Croquettes ......................................................... 13
(Bolinho de Queijo) ......................................................... 13
Brazilian-style Potato Salad (Majionese de Patatas) ...... 15
Tropical Cobb Salad (Salata Tropical) ............................ 17
Black Eye Pea Fritters ..................................................... 19
(Acaraje de Bahia) .......................................................... 19
Fried Chicken Pastries .................................................... 21
(Pastel de Frango Com Catupiry) ................................... 21
Cheese Bread (Pao de Queijo) ....................................... 23
Brazilian Chicken Salad (Salpicao) ................................. 25

**SOUPS AND STEWS**     **27**
Black Bean Stew with Smoked Meats (Feijoada
Completa) ....................................................................... 27
Brazilian Beef Stew ......................................................... 29
(Picadinho de Carne) ...................................................... 29
Heart of Palm Soup ......................................................... 31
Beef Stew in Clay Pot (Barreado) ................................... 35
Black Bean Soup ............................................................. 37
(Caldinho de Carne) ........................................................ 37
Coconut Butternut Squash Soup (Sopa e Abobora e
Coco) ............................................................................... 39
Cream Corn Soup ........................................................... 41
(Creme de Milho Verde) .................................................. 41
Leao Veloso Seafood Soup ............................................ 43
Shrimp Stew (Vatapa) ..................................................... 43

**MAIN ENTRÉES**     **45**
Beef Rump Steak BBQ ................................................... 45

(Picanha with Farofa) ..................................................... 45
Brazilian BBQ (Churrasco) ............................................. 47
Brazilian Chicken Pot Pie (Empadao de Frango) ........... 48
Roasted Pork Loin (Lombo Assado) .............................. 51
Brazilian Marinated Chicken .......................................... 53
Grilled Chicken Leg Wrapped in Bacon ........................ 55
(Churrasco de Frango com Bacon) ............................... 55
Ground Beef Kebab ....................................................... 57
(Kafta no Espeto) ........................................................... 57
Bahian Style Coconut Chicken (Moqueca de Frango) .... 59
Baked Salt Cod with Onions, Peppers, and Potatoes ..... 61
(Bacalhau Ao Forno) ...................................................... 61
Fish Baked in Banana Leaves (Peixena Folha de
Bananeira) ...................................................................... 63
Shrimp Bobo (Bobo de Camarao) .................................. 65
Chicken Skewers with Pineapple and Bacon ................. 67
(Espetinho de Frango com Bacon) ................................ 67
Bahian Seafood Stew ..................................................... 68
(Mequeca de Peixe Baiana) ........................................... 68
Crazy Beef Sandwich ..................................................... 70
(Sanduiche de Carne Louca) ......................................... 70

**VEGETARIAN, SIDES, BEANS AND RICE**     **73**
Vegetarian Bobo ............................................................ 73
(Bobo Vegetariano) ........................................................ 73
Heart of Palm Bahian Stew (Moqueca de Palmito) ........ 75
Farofa with Plantains ...................................................... 77
(Farofa de Banana) ........................................................ 77
Farofa with Fried Bacon ................................................. 79
Everyday Black Beans ................................................... 81
(Feijao Preto) .................................................................. 81
Coconut Beans (Feijao de Coco) ................................... 83
Black Beans and Rice .................................................... 84
(Feijao de Feijao Preto) .................................................. 84
Rice, Beans, and Sausages ........................................... 85
(Feijao Com Linguica) .................................................... 85
Brazilian Rice (Arroz Brasileiro) ..................................... 87
Black Eye Peas and Rice ............................................... 89
(Baiao de Dois) ............................................................... 89

**DESSERTS** **91**
    Chocolate Truffles (Brigadeiros) ......................................91
    Grilled Spiced Pineapple ..................................................93
    (Abacaxi Grelhado) .........................................................93
    Coconut Custard (Quindim) ............................................95
    Brazilian-Style Churros ...................................................97
    Coconut Tapioca Pudding ...............................................99
    (Cuscuz de Tapioca) .......................................................99
    Coconut Sweet (Queijadinha) .......................................101
    Passion Fruit Mousse ....................................................103
    (Mousse de Maracuja) ..................................................103

# COOKING CONVERSION CHARTS

1. **Measuring Equivalent Chart**

| Type | Imperial | Imperial | Metric |
|---|---|---|---|
| Weight | 1 dry ounce | | 28 g |
| | 1 pound | 16 dry ounces | 0.45 kg |
| Volume | 1 teaspoon | | 5 ml |
| | 1 dessert spoon | 2 teaspoons | 10 ml |
| | 1 tablespoon | 3 teaspoons | 15 ml |
| | 1 Australian tablespoon | 4 teaspoons | 20 ml |
| | 1 fluid ounce | 2 tablespoons | 30 ml |
| | 1 cup | 16 tablespoons | 240 ml |
| | 1 cup | 8 fluid ounces | 240 ml |
| | 1 pint | 2 cups | 470 ml |
| | 1 quart | 2 pints | 0.95 l |
| | 1 gallon | 4 quarts | 3.8 l |
| Length | 1 inch | | 2.54 cm |

\* Numbers are rounded to the closest equivalent

2. **Oven Temperature Equivalent Chart**

| Fahrenheit (°F) | Celsius (°C) | Gas Mark |
|---|---|---|
| 220 | 100 | |
| 225 | 110 | 1/4 |
| 250 | 120 | 1/2 |
| 275 | 140 | 1 |
| 300 | 150 | 2 |
| 325 | 160 | 3 |
| 350 | 180 | 4 |
| 375 | 190 | 5 |
| 400 | 200 | 6 |
| 425 | 220 | 7 |
| 450 | 230 | 8 |
| 475 | 250 | 9 |
| 500 | 260 | |

\* Celsius (°C) = T (°F)-32] \* 5/9
\*\* Fahrenheit (°F) = T (°C) \* 9/5 + 32
\*\*\* Numbers are rounded to the closest equivalent

In the same series:

**Image Credits**

*Brazilian Chicken Salad (Salpicao)* - By Luiz Fernando Reis from Rio de Janeiro, Brasil - Delicia 01, CC BY 2.0, https://commons.wikimedia.org/w/index.php?curid=85393971

*Black Bean Stew with Smoked Meats (Feijoada Completa)* - Andre Rebeiro [CC BY (https://creativecommons.org/licenses/by/2.0)]

*Shrimp Stew (Vatapa)* - By Elingunnur - Own work, CC BY 3.0, https://commons.wikimedia.org/w/index.php?curid=6040752

*Shrimp Bobo (Bobo de Camarao)* - By Victorgrigas - Own work, CC BY-SA 3.0, https://commons.wikimedia.org/w/index.php?curid=18760880

*Bahian Seafood Stew (Mequeca de Peixe Baiana)* - By Gilrovina, CC BY-SA 4.0, https://commons.wikimedia.org/w/index.php?curid=61595941

*Black Eye Peas and Rice (Baiao de Dois)* - By Zé Carlos Barretta, CC BY 2.0, https://commons.wikimedia.org/w/index.php?curid=38019917

Printed in Great Britain
by Amazon